COUNTRY
Soups

Publications International, Ltd.

Favorite Brand Name Recipes at www.fbnr.com

Pictured on the front cover: Confetti Chicken Chili *(page 128)*.
Pictured on the back cover *(top to bottom):* Tomato-Basil Crab Bisque *(page 114)* and
Creamy Turkey and Veggie Soup with Cream *(page 26)*.

ISBN-13: 978-1-4127-9787-0
ISBN-10: 1-4127-9787-X

Library of Congress Control Number: 2009921344

Manufactured in China.

8 7 6 5 4 3 2 1

Microwave Cooking: Microwave ovens vary in wattage. Use the cooking times as
guidelines and check for doneness before adding more time.

Preparation/Cooking Times: Preparation times are based on the approximate
amount of time required to assemble the recipe before cooking, baking, chilling or
serving. These times include preparation steps such as measuring, chopping and mixing.
The fact that some preparations and cooking can be done simultaneously is taken into
account. Preparation of optional ingredients and serving suggestions is not included.

Table of Contents

*** *** ***

Beef & Pork

✳ ✳ ✳

Beefy Broccoli & Cheese Soup

  2 cups chicken broth
  1 package (10 ounces) frozen chopped broccoli, thawed
  ¼ cup chopped onion
  ¼ pound ground beef
  1 cup milk
  2 tablespoons all-purpose flour
  1 cup (4 ounces) shredded sharp Cheddar cheese
1½ teaspoons chopped fresh oregano *or* ½ teaspoon dried oregano
    Salt and black pepper
    Hot pepper sauce

1. Bring broth to a boil in medium saucepan. Add broccoli and onion; cook 5 minutes or until broccoli is tender.

2. Meanwhile, brown beef in small skillet 6 to 8 minutes over medium-high heat, stirring to break up meat. Drain fat. Gradually stir milk into flour in small bowl until well blended. Add milk mixture and ground beef to broccoli mixture; cook, stirring constantly, until mixture is thickened and bubbly.

3. Add cheese and oregano; stir until cheese is melted. Season to taste with salt, pepper and pepper sauce. *Makes 4 to 5 servings*

Beef, Lentil and Onion Soup

  1 tablespoon olive oil
  ¾ pound lean boneless beef stew meat, cut into 1-inch pieces
  2 cups chopped carrots
  1 cup sliced celery
  1 cup dried lentils, rinsed and sorted
  2 teaspoons dried thyme
  ¼ teaspoon black pepper
  ⅛ teaspoon salt
3¼ cups water
  1 can (about 10 ounces) condensed French onion soup, undiluted

Slow Cooker Directions

1. Heat oil in large skillet over medium-high heat. Add beef; cook until browned on all sides.

2. Layer carrots, celery, lentils and beef in slow cooker. Sprinkle with thyme, pepper and salt. Pour water and soup into slow cooker.

3. Cover; cook on LOW 7 to 8 hours or HIGH 3½ to 4 hours or until meat and lentils are tender. *Makes 4 servings*

Tip

Because slow cookers cook at a low heat for a long time, they are perfect for dishes calling for less tender cuts of meat.

Veggie Beef Skillet Soup

¾ **pound ground beef**
1 **tablespoon olive oil**
2 **cups coarsely chopped cabbage**
1 **cup chopped green bell pepper**
2 **cups water**
1 **can (about 14 ounces) stewed tomatoes**
1 **cup frozen mixed vegetables**
⅓ **cup ketchup**
1 **tablespoon beef bouillon granules**
2 **teaspoons Worcestershire sauce**
2 **teaspoons balsamic vinegar**
⅛ **teaspoon red pepper flakes**
¼ **cup chopped fresh parsley**

1. Brown beef in large skillet over medium-high heat 6 to 8 minutes, stirring to break up meat. Drain fat.

2. Heat oil in same skillet. Add cabbage and bell pepper; cook and stir 4 minutes or until cabbage is wilted. Add beef, water, tomatoes, mixed vegetables, ketchup, bouillon, Worcestershire sauce, vinegar and pepper flakes; bring to a boil. Reduce heat; cover and simmer 20 minutes.

3. Remove from heat; let stand 5 minutes. Stir in parsley before serving.

Makes 4 servings

Tip

Browning is the technique of cooking food quickly until the surface is brown. Browning meats and vegetables gives soups and stews a richer flavor and aroma.

Ham, Potato & Cabbage Soup

1 tablespoon vegetable oil

1 large sweet onion, chopped (about 2 cups)

1 clove garlic, minced

6 cups SWANSON® Chicken Broth (Regular, Natural Goodness™ *or* Certified Organic)

¼ teaspoon ground black pepper

3 cups shredded cabbage

1 large potato, diced (about 2 cups)

½ of an 8-ounce cooked ham steak, cut into 2-inch-long strips (about 1 cup)

2 tablespoons chopped fresh parsley

1 teaspoon caraway seed (optional)

1. Heat the oil in a 6-quart saucepot over medium-high heat. Add the onion and garlic and cook for 3 minutes or until tender.

2. Stir in the broth, black pepper, cabbage, potato and ham. Heat to a boil. Reduce the heat to medium-low. Cover and cook for 20 minutes or until the potato is tender.

3. Stir in the parsley and caraway seed, if desired.   *Makes 6 servings*

Kitchen Tip: A small head of cabbage, about 1 pound, will be enough for the amount of cabbage needed for this recipe.

Prep Time: 15 minutes
Cook Time: 30 minutes

Beef and Beet Borscht

2 cans (15 ounces each) sliced beets
1 cup buttermilk
⅛ teaspoon black pepper
⅛ teaspoon ground cloves
1 cup reduced-sodium beef broth
4 ounces thinly sliced deli rare roast beef, cut into short thin strips
¼ cup sour cream
   Chopped parsley (optional)

1. Drain beets, reserving 1 cup liquid. Place half of beets in food processor; process until finely chopped. Add buttermilk, pepper and cloves; process until smooth. Transfer to medium bowl.

2. Stir in remaining beets, broth, reserved liquid and roast beef. Cover; chill at least 2 hours or up to 24 hours. Ladle into bowls; top with sour cream and sprinkle with parsley. *Makes 4 servings*

Hamburger Veggie Soup

1 pound ground beef
1 bag (16 ounces) frozen mixed vegetables
1 package (10 ounces) frozen seasoning blend vegetables
1 can (about 14 ounces) stewed tomatoes, undrained
2 cans (5½ ounces each) spicy vegetable juice
1 can (10¾ ounces) condensed tomato soup, undiluted
   Salt and black pepper

Slow Cooker Directions

1. Brown beef in large skillet over medium-high heat 6 to 8 minutes, stirring to break up meat. Drain fat.

2. Combine beef, vegetables, tomatoes, juice and soup in slow cooker. Stir well.

3. Cover; cook on HIGH 4 hours. Season to taste with salt and pepper. *Makes 4 to 6 servings*

Beef and Beet Borscht

Sausage Vegetable Rotini Soup

1 tablespoon olive oil
6 ounces bulk pork sausage
1 cup chopped onion
1 cup chopped green bell pepper
3 cups water
1 can (about 14 ounces) diced tomatoes
¼ cup ketchup
2 teaspoons beef bouillon granules
2 teaspoons chili powder
4 ounces uncooked tri-colored rotini pasta
1 cup frozen corn, thawed and drained

1. Heat oil in large saucepan over medium-high heat. Add sausage; cook 3 minutes or until no longer pink, stirring to break up sausage. Drain fat. Add onion and bell pepper; cook and stir 3 to 4 minutes or until onion is translucent.

2. Add water, tomatoes, ketchup, bouillon and chili powder; bring to a boil over high heat. Stir in pasta; return to a boil. Reduce heat to medium-low; simmer, uncovered, 12 minutes. Stir in corn; cook 2 minutes or until pasta is tender and corn is heated through. *Makes 4 servings*

Beef Soup with Vegetables

- 1 pound boneless beef round steak, cut into 1-inch cubes
  Black pepper
- 2 tablespoons all-purpose flour
- 2 tablespoons vegetable oil
- 3 medium onions, chopped (about 3 cups)
- 4 cloves garlic, minced
- 1 tablespoon chopped fresh thyme or 1 teaspoon dried thyme leaves, crushed
- 12 small red-skinned potatoes, cut into quarters
- 2 medium carrots, sliced (about 1 cup)
- 4 cups SWANSON® Beef Broth (Regular, 50% Less Sodium *or* Certified Organic)
- 2 tablespoons tomato paste
  Sour cream (optional)
  Chopped green onions (optional)

1. Season beef with pepper and coat with flour. Heat the oil in a 10-inch skillet over medium-high heat. Add the beef and cooked until it's well browned, stirring often.

2. Place onions, garlic, thyme, potatoes and carrots in a 3½-quart slow cooker. Top with browned beef. Stir **1 cup** of the broth and tomato paste in a small bowl. Pour the broth mixture and remaining broth into the cooker.

3. Cover and cook on LOW for 8 to 10 hours* or until the meat is fork-tender. Serve with sour cream and onions, if desired.   *Makes 6 servings*

Or on HIGH for 4 to 5 hours

Prep Time: 20 minutes
Cook Time: 8 to 10 hours (LOW) • 4 to 5 hours (HIGH)

Pork and Cabbage Soup

½ pound pork loin, cut into ½-inch cubes
1 medium onion, chopped
2 slices bacon, finely chopped
2 cups reduced-sodium beef broth
2 cups reduced-sodium chicken broth
1 can (about 28 ounces) whole tomatoes, drained and coarsely chopped
2 medium carrots, sliced
¾ teaspoon dried marjoram
1 bay leaf
⅛ teaspoon black pepper
¼ medium cabbage, chopped
2 tablespoons chopped fresh parsley

1. Heat Dutch oven over medium heat until hot; add pork, onion and bacon. Cook and stir until meat is no longer pink and onion is slightly tender. Drain fat.

2. Stir in beef broth, chicken broth, tomatoes, carrots, marjoram, bay leaf and pepper; bring to a boil over high heat. Reduce heat to medium-low; simmer, uncovered, about 30 minutes. Remove and discard bay leaf. Skim off fat.

3. Add cabbage; bring to a boil over high heat. Reduce heat to medium-low; simmer, uncovered, about 15 minutes or until cabbage is tender. Stir in parsley.   *Makes 6 servings*

Kansas City Steak Soup

½ **pound ground beef**
3 **cups frozen mixed vegetables**
2 **cups water**
1 **can (about 14 ounces) stewed tomatoes, undrained**
1 **cup chopped onion**
1 **cup sliced celery**
1 **beef bouillon cube**
½ **to 1 teaspoon black pepper**
1 **can (about 14 ounces) reduced-sodium beef broth**
½ **cup all-purpose flour**

1. Brown beef in large saucepan over medium-high heat 6 to 8 minutes, stirring to break up meat. Drain fat.

2. Add mixed vegetables, water, tomatoes with juice, onion, celery, bouillon cube and pepper; bring to a boil. Whisk together broth and flour in small bowl until smooth; add to beef mixture, stirring constantly. Return mixture to a boil. Reduce heat to low; cover and simmer 15 minutes, stirring frequently. *Makes 6 servings*

Tip

If time permits, allow the soup to simmer an additional 30 minutes to blend the flavors.

Sausage & Vegetable Soup

1 can (about 15 ounces) black beans, rinsed and drained
1 can (about 14 ounces) diced tomatoes
1 can (10¾ ounces) condensed cream of mushroom soup,
   undiluted
½ pound sausage, cut into ½-inch slices
2 cups diced potato
1 cup chopped onion
1 cup chopped red bell pepper
½ cup water
2 teaspoons horseradish
2 teaspoons honey
1 teaspoon dried basil

Slow Cooker Directions
Combine all ingredients in slow cooker; mix well. Cover; cook on
LOW 7 to 8 hours or until potato is tender.   *Makes 6 to 8 servings*

Tip

Keep the lid on! The slow cooker can take as
long as 30 minutes to regain heat lost when
the cover is removed. Only remove the cover
if instructed to do so by the recipe.

Chicken & Poultry

* * *

Chicken & Barley Soup

1 cup thinly sliced celery

1 medium onion, coarsely chopped

1 carrot, thinly sliced

½ cup uncooked medium pearled barley

1 clove garlic, minced

1 cut-up whole chicken (about 3 pounds)

1 tablespoon olive oil

2½ cups chicken broth

1 can (about 14 ounces) diced tomatoes

¾ teaspoon salt

½ teaspoon dried basil

¼ teaspoon black pepper

Slow Cooker Directions

1. Place celery, onion, carrot, barley and garlic in slow cooker.

2. Remove and discard skin from chicken pieces. Separate drumsticks from thighs. Trim back bone from breasts. Save wings for another use. Heat oil in large skillet over medium-high heat; brown chicken pieces on all sides. Place chicken in slow cooker.

3. Add broth, tomatoes, salt, basil and pepper to slow cooker. Cover; cook on LOW 7 to 8 hours or HIGH 4 hours or until chicken and barley are tender. Remove chicken from slow cooker; separate chicken from bones. Cut chicken into bite-size pieces, discarding bones; stir chicken into soup.

Makes 4 servings

Sausage & Rice Soup

2 tablespoons butter or margarine

1 large or 2 medium leeks, white and light green parts sliced

2 carrots, thinly sliced

1 package (16 ounces) JENNIE-O Turkey Store® Extra Lean
   Smoked Sausage

2 cups diced mixed bell peppers, preferably red and yellow

3½ cups reduced-sodium chicken broth

1 cup water

¾ cup quick-cooking brown rice, uncooked

½ teaspoon dried sage

¼ teaspoon freshly ground black pepper

   Chopped fresh chives (optional)

1. Melt butter in large saucepan over medium heat. Add leeks and carrots; cook 5 minutes, stirring occasionally.

2. Meanwhile, cut sausage into ½-inch slices; remove and discard casings, if desired. Add sausage to saucepan; cook 5 minutes, stirring occasionally. Add bell peppers, broth, water, rice, sage and pepper; bring to a boil over high heat.

3. Reduce heat; simmer uncovered 15 minutes or until rice is tender. Ladle into bowls; top with chives, if desired. *Makes 6 servings*

Tip

To remove a sausage casing, use a paring knife to slit the casing at one end. Be careful not to cut through the sausage. Grasp the cut edge and gently pull the casing away from the sausage.

Country Turkey and Veggie Soup with Cream

2 tablespoons butter, divided
8 ounces sliced mushrooms
½ cup chopped onion
½ cup thinly sliced celery
1 medium red bell pepper, chopped
1 medium carrot, thinly sliced
½ teaspoon dried thyme
4 cups reduced-sodium chicken or turkey broth
4 ounces uncooked egg noodles
2 cups chopped cooked turkey
1 cup half-and-half
½ cup frozen green peas, thawed
¾ teaspoon salt

Slow Cooker Directions

1. Melt 1 tablespoon butter in large nonstick skillet over medium-high heat. Add mushrooms and onion; cook and stir 4 minutes or until onion is translucent. Transfer mixture to slow cooker.

2. Add celery, bell pepper, carrot and thyme to slow cooker; pour in broth. Cover; cook on HIGH 2½ hours.

3. Add noodles and turkey. Cover; cook 20 minutes. Stir in half-and-half, peas, remaining 1 tablespoon butter and salt. Cook until noodles are tender and soup is heated through. *Makes 8 servings*

Chicken & Herb Dumplings

2 pounds skinless, boneless chicken breasts *and/or* thighs, cut into 1-inch pieces

5 medium carrots, cut into 1-inch pieces (about 2½ cups)

4 stalks celery, cut into 1-inch pieces (about 2 cups)

2 cups frozen whole kernel corn

3½ cups SWANSON® Chicken Broth (Regular, Natural Goodness™ *or* Certified Organic)

¼ teaspoon black pepper

¼ cup all-purpose flour

½ cup water

2 cups all-purpose baking mix

⅔ cup milk

1 tablespoon chopped fresh rosemary leaves *or* 1 teaspoon dried rosemary leaves, crushed

1. Stir the chicken, carrots, celery, corn, broth and black pepper in a 6-quart slow cooker.

2. Cover and cook on LOW for 7 to 8 hours* or until the chicken is cooked through.

3. Stir the flour and water in a small bowl until the mixture is smooth. Stir the flour mixture in the cooker. Turn the heat to HIGH. Cover and cook for 5 minutes or until the mixture boils and thickens.

4. Stir the baking mix, milk and rosemary in a medium bowl. Drop the batter by rounded tablespoonfuls over the chicken mixture. Tilt the lid to vent and cook on HIGH for 40 minutes or until the dumplings are cooked in the center.   *Makes 8 servings*

Or on HIGH for 4 to 5 hours.

Kitchen Tip: Leaving the lid slightly ajar prevents condensation from dripping onto the dumplings during cooking.

Prep Time: 20 minutes
Cook Time: 7 hours, 45 minutes

Chicken Tortellini Soup

2 tablespoons olive oil
4 boneless, skinless chicken breast halves, cut in bite-size pieces
2 ribs celery, cut in ¼-inch slices
1 medium carrot, cut ¼-inch slices
1 medium onion, diced
2 cloves garlic, minced
6 cups reduced-sodium chicken broth
2 cups water
1 can (14½ ounces) diced tomatoes
2 small zucchini, halved lengthwise, cut in ½-inch slices
½ teaspoon pepper
½ teaspoon Italian seasoning
1 package (9 ounces) plain or spinach cheese-filled tortellini
  Salt to taste
  Freshly grated Parmesan cheese

In 5-quart saucepan or Dutch oven, place oil and heat to medium-high temperature. Add chicken, celery, carrot, onion and garlic; cook, stirring, about 8 minutes or until chicken is lightly browned and vegetables are tender-crisp. Add broth, water, tomatoes, zucchini, pepper and Italian seasoning. Heat to boiling; reduce heat, cover and cook 7 minutes. Return to boiling, add tortellini and cook 7 minutes or until tortellini is done. Serve in individual bowls; top with sprinkle of Parmesan cheese. *Makes 6 servings*

Favorite recipe from ***Delmarva Poultry Industry, Inc.***

Roasted Corn and Chicken Soup

4 tablespoons olive oil, divided
1 can (15 ounces) yellow corn, drained
1 can (15 ounces) white corn, drained
1 onion, diced
3 tablespoons ORTEGA® Diced Green Chiles
½ of (1½- to 2-pound) cooked rotisserie chicken, shredded
1 packet (1.25 ounces) Ortega® Taco Seasoning Mix
4 cups chicken broth
4 Ortega® Yellow Corn Taco Shells, crumbled

1. Heat 2 tablespoons olive oil over medium heat in large skillet. Add corn. Cook and stir until brown, about 8 minutes. Add remaining 2 tablespoons olive oil, onion and chiles. Cook and stir 3 minutes longer.

2. Transfer mixture to large pot. Stir in shredded chicken. Add seasoning mix and toss to combine. Stir in chicken broth and bring to a boil. Reduce heat to low. Simmer 15 minutes. Serve with crumbled taco shells.

Makes 8 servings

Creamy Turkey Soup

2 cans (10¾ ounces each) condensed cream of chicken soup, undiluted
2 cups chopped cooked turkey breast
1 package (8 ounces) sliced mushrooms
1 medium yellow onion, chopped
1 teaspoon rubbed sage *or* ½ teaspoon dried poultry seasoning
1 cup frozen peas, thawed
½ cup milk
1 jar (about 4 ounces) diced pimiento

Slow Cooker Directions

1. Combine soup, turkey, mushrooms, onion and sage in slow cooker. Cover; cook on LOW 8 hours or on HIGH 4 hours.

2. Stir in peas, milk and pimiento. Cover; cook on HIGH 15 minutes or until heated through.

Makes 5 to 6 servings

Roasted Corn and Chicken Soup

Chile Verde Chicken Stew

⅓ cup all-purpose flour
1½ teaspoons salt, divided
¼ teaspoon black pepper
1½ pounds boneless skinless chicken breasts, cut into 1½-inch cubes
4 tablespoons vegetable oil, divided
1 pound tomatillos (about 9), husked and halved
2 medium onions, chopped
2 cans (4 ounces each) mild green chiles
1 tablespoon dried oregano
1 tablespoon ground cumin
2 cloves garlic, chopped
1 teaspoon sugar
2 cups reduced-sodium chicken broth
8 ounces Mexican lager
5 red potatoes, diced
    Chopped fresh cilantro, sour cream, shredded Monterey Jack cheese, lime wedges, diced avocado and/or hot pepper sauce (optional)

1. Combine flour, 1 teaspoon salt and pepper in large bowl. Add chicken; toss to coat. Heat 2 tablespoons oil in large nonstick skillet over medium heat. Add chicken; cook until lightly browned on all sides. Transfer chicken to Dutch oven.

2. Heat remaining 2 tablespoons oil in same skillet. Stir in tomatillos, onions, green chiles, oregano, cumin, garlic, sugar and remaining ½ teaspoon salt. Cook over medium heat 20 minutes or until vegetables are softened, stirring frequently. Stir in broth and beer. Process mixture in batches in food processor or blender until almost smooth.

3. Add mixture to chicken in Dutch over; stir in potatoes. Cover and bring to a boil over medium-high heat. Reduce heat to low; simmer, stirring occasionally, 1 hour or until potatoes are tender. Season to taste with salt and pepper.

4. Serve in shallow bowls with desired toppings.   *Makes 6 servings*

Variation: Omit potatoes and serve over rice.

Rich and Hearty Drumstick Soup

2 turkey drumsticks (about 1¾ pounds total)
3 carrots, peeled and sliced
3 stalks celery, thinly sliced
1 onion, chopped
2 cloves garlic, minced
1 teaspoon poultry seasoning
4 cups reduced-sodium chicken broth
3 cups water
8 ounces uncooked egg noodles
⅓ cup chopped parsley
   Salt and black pepper

Slow Cooker Directions

1. Place drumsticks, carrots, celery, onion, garlic and poultry seasoning in slow cooker; pour in broth and water. Cover; cook on HIGH 5 hours or until meat is falling off bones.

2. Remove turkey; set aside. Add noodles. Cover; cook 30 minutes more or until noodles are tender. Meanwhile, remove and discard skin and bones from turkey; shred meat.

3. Return turkey to slow cooker. Cover and cook until turkey is warmed through. Stir in parsley. Season to taste with salt and pepper.

Makes 8 servings

Spaghetti Soup

2 tablespoons vegetable oil

½ pound skinless, boneless chicken breast halves, cut into cubes

1 medium onion, chopped (about ½ cup)

1 large carrot, chopped (about ½ cup)

1 stalk celery, finely chopped (about ½ cup)

2 cloves garlic, minced

4 cups SWANSON® Chicken Broth (Regular, Natural Goodness™ *or* Certified Organic)

1 can (10¾ ounces) CAMPBELL'S® Condensed Tomato Soup Regular, Healthy Request® *or* 25% Less Sodium)

1 cup water

3 ounces uncooked spaghetti, broken into 1-inch pieces

2 tablespoons chopped fresh parsley (optional)

1. Heat **1 tablespoon** oil in a 6-quart saucepot over medium-high heat. Add the chicken and cook until it's well browned, stirring often. Remove the chicken from the saucepot.

2. Add the remaining oil to the saucepot and heat over medium heat. Add the onion and cook for 1 minute. Add the carrots and cook for 1 minute. Add the celery and garlic and cook for 1 minute.

3. Stir in the broth, soup and water. Heat to a boil. Stir in the pasta. Cook for 10 minutes or until the pasta is tender. Stir in the chicken and parsley, if desired, and cook until the mixture is hot and bubbling.   *Makes 4 servings*

Prep Time: 15 minutes
Cook Time: 30 minutes

Chicken and Wild Rice Soup

½ cup uncooked wild rice
5 cups reduced-sodium chicken broth, divided
¼ cup (½ stick) butter
1 large carrot, sliced
1 medium onion, chopped
2 stalks celery, chopped
¼ pound fresh mushrooms, sliced
2 tablespoons all-purpose flour
¼ teaspoon salt
¼ teaspoon white pepper
1½ cups chopped cooked chicken
¼ cup dry sherry

1. Rinse rice thoroughly in fine strainer under cold running water; drain.

2. Combine 2½ cups broth and rice in medium saucepan. Bring to a boil over medium-high heat. Reduce heat to low; cover and simmer 1 hour or until rice is tender. Drain; set aside.

3. Melt butter in large saucepan over medium heat. Add carrot; cook and stir 3 minutes. Add onion, celery and mushrooms; cook and stir 3 to 4 minutes until vegetables are tender. Remove from heat. Whisk in flour, salt and pepper until smooth.

4. Gradually stir in remaining 2½ cups broth. Bring to a boil over medium heat; cook and stir 1 minute or until thickened. Stir in chicken and sherry. Reduce heat to low; simmer, uncovered, 3 minutes or until heated through.

5. Spoon ¼ cup cooked rice into each serving bowl. Ladle soup over rice.

Makes 4 to 6 servings

Chicken and Wild Rice Soup

Potato Chicken Soup

2½ pounds DOLE® Red Potatoes, peeled, cut into 1-inch cubes
½ pound DOLE® Peeled Mini Carrots, halved
4 cups reduced-sodium chicken broth
½ bay leaf
2 teaspoons olive oil
1 small onion, cut into 1-inch cubes
1 teaspoon dried tarragon leaves, crushed
¼ teaspoon dried thyme leaves, crushed
1½ cups cooked diced chicken
1 to 2 tablespoons minced parsley
⅛ teaspoon salt

• Combine potatoes, carrots, chicken broth and bay leaf in large pot. Bring to boil; reduce heat and simmer 15 to 20 minutes.

• Heat oil in nonstick skillet. Add onion; cook 6 to 8 minutes or until lightly browned. Add tarragon and thyme; cook 30 seconds.

• Add onion mixture, chicken, parsley and salt to soup in pot. Cook 5 minutes longer or until heated through. Remove bay leaf before serving.

Makes 4 servings

Prep Time: 25 minutes
Cook Time: 35 minutes

Curried Turkey Noodle Soup

1 tablespoon olive oil
¾ pound turkey breast tenderloin, cut into bite-size pieces
5 cups water
2 packages (3 ounces each) chicken-flavored ramen noodles
1 tablespoon curry powder
⅛ teaspoon salt
1 cup sliced celery
1 medium apple, cored and chopped (1½ cups)
¼ cup unsalted dry roasted peanuts

1. Heat oil in large saucepan over medium-high heat. Add turkey; cook and stir 3 to 4 minutes or until no longer pink. Remove turkey; set aside.

2. Add water, flavor packets from noodles, curry powder and salt to saucepan; bring to a boil. Reduce heat; cover and simmer 5 minutes.

3. Break up noodles; gently stir noodles and celery into saucepan. Bring mixture to a boil. Reduce heat and simmer, uncovered, 5 minutes.

4. Stir in turkey and apple. Cook until heated through. Ladle into bowls; sprinkle with peanuts.

Makes 5 servings

Tip

Curry powder adds an exotic touch to all kinds of foods including baked goods, soups, vegetables and more. Be sure to start with a light touch as this spice gets hotter the longer it stands.

Green Chile Chicken Soup with Tortilla Dumplings

8 ORTEGA® Taco Shells, broken
½ cup water
⅓ cup milk
2 onions, diced, divided
1 egg
½ teaspoon POLANER® Minced Garlic
1 tablespoon olive oil
4 cups reduced-sodium chicken broth
2 cups shredded cooked chicken
2 tablespoons ORTEGA® Roasted Chiles
¼ cup vegetable oil

1. Place taco shells, water, milk, 1 diced onion, egg and garlic in blender or food processor. Pulse several times to crush taco shells and blend ingredients. Pour into medium bowl; let stand 10 minutes to thicken.

2. Heat 1 tablespoon olive oil in saucepan over medium heat. Add remaining diced onion; cook and stir 4 minutes or until translucent. Stir in broth, chicken and chiles. Reduce heat to a simmer.

3. Heat ¼ cup vegetable oil in small skillet over medium heat. Form taco shell mixture into 1-inch balls. Drop into hot oil in batches. Cook dumplings about 3 minutes or until browned. Turn over and continue cooking 3 minutes longer or until browned. Remove dumplings; drain on paper towels. Add dumplings to soup just before serving. *Makes 4 to 6 servings*

Tip: For an even more authentic Mexican flavor, garnish the soup with fresh chopped cilantro and a squirt of lime juice.

Tip: For ease of preparation, purchase a cooked rotisserie chicken from your supermarket's hot deli case.

Prep Time: 15 minutes
Start to Finish: 30 minutes

Green Chile Chicken Soup with Tortilla Dumplings

Spicy Squash & Chicken Soup

1 tablespoon vegetable oil
1 small onion, finely chopped
1 stalk celery, finely chopped
2 cups delicata or butternut squash (1 small squash), cut into
    1-inch cubes
2 cups chicken broth
1 can (about 14 ounces) diced tomatoes, undrained (see Note)
1 cup chopped cooked chicken
½ teaspoon ground ginger
¼ teaspoon salt
⅛ teaspoon ground cumin
⅛ teaspoon black pepper
2 teaspoons fresh lime juice
1 tablespoon minced fresh cilantro (optional)

1. Heat oil in large saucepan over medium heat. Add onion and celery; cook and stir 5 minutes or just until tender. Stir in squash, broth, tomatoes, chicken, ginger, salt, cumin and pepper; mix well.

2. Cover; cook over low heat 30 minutes or until squash is tender. Stir in lime juice. Sprinkle with cilantro, if desired. *Makes 4 servings*

Note: For extra-spicy soup, use diced tomatoes with chiles.

Turkey and Rice Soup

2 cups JENNIE-O Turkey Store® Turkey, cooked, cut in bite-size pieces
8 cups water
2 stalks celery, sliced
1 onion, chopped
3 chicken bouillon cubes
¼ teaspoon poultry seasoning
1 bay leaf
¾ cup uncooked long-grain rice
2 carrots, peeled and sliced

1. Combine first 7 ingredients in 2½-quart saucepan. Bring to a boil; cover, reduce heat and simmer 40 minutes.

2. Add rice and carrots; cover and simmer additional 20 minutes or until rice is tender. Remove bay leaf before serving.   *Makes 4 servings*

Chicken and Homemade Noodle Soup

¾ cup all-purpose flour
2 teaspoons minced fresh thyme *or* ½ teaspoon dried thyme, divided
¼ teaspoon salt
1 egg yolk, beaten
2 cups plus 3 tablespoons cold water, divided
1 pound boneless skinless chicken thighs, cut into ½-inch pieces
5 cups chicken broth
1 medium onion, chopped
1 medium carrot, thinly sliced
¾ cup frozen peas
Chopped fresh parsley

1. To prepare noodles, stir together flour, 1 teaspoon thyme and salt in small bowl. Add egg yolk and 3 tablespoons water; stir until well blended. Shape into ball. Place dough on lightly floured surface; flatten slightly. Knead 5 minutes or until dough is smooth and elastic, adding more flour to prevent sticking if necessary. Cover with plastic wrap; let stand 15 minutes.

2. Roll out dough to ⅛-inch thickness on lightly floured surface. If dough is too elastic, let rest a few minutes. Let dough stand about 30 minutes to dry slightly. Cut into ¼-inch-wide strips. Cut strips 1½ to 2 inches long; set aside.

3. Combine chicken and remaining 2 cups water in medium saucepan. Bring to a boil over high heat. Reduce heat to medium-low; cover and simmer 5 minutes or until chicken is no longer pink. Drain chicken.

4. Combine broth, onion, carrot and remaining 1 teaspoon thyme in Dutch oven or large saucepan. Bring to a boil over high heat. Add noodles. Reduce heat to medium-low; simmer, uncovered, 8 minutes or until noodles are tender. Stir in chicken and peas; bring to a boil. Remove from heat. Sprinkle with parsley.
Makes 4 servings

Creamy Chicken and Brown Rice Soup

3¼ cups reduced-sodium chicken broth

1 can (12 ounces) evaporated milk

¼ cup cornstarch

1 teaspoon poultry seasoning

6 ounces cooked chicken breast, diced

1 cup frozen mixed vegetables, thawed

2 cups cooked SUCCESS®, MAHATMA®, CAROLINA® or
   RICELAND® Whole Grain Brown Rice

Salt and black pepper, optional

1. In a large pot, bring chicken broth and evaporated milk to a boil. In a small cup, dissolve cornstarch and poultry seasoning with ¼ cup water and stir into hot broth. Stir constantly for 1 minute; reduce heat to low and stir in diced chicken and vegetables.

2. Continue to simmer 5 minutes. Stir in rice. Season with salt and pepper, if desired.
Makes 6 servings

Vegetables & Grains

* * *

Italian Skillet Roasted Vegetable Soup

1 tablespoon olive oil

1 medium red, yellow or orange bell pepper, chopped

1 clove garlic, minced

2 cups water

1 can (about 14 ounces) fire-roasted or diced tomatoes

1 medium zucchini, thinly sliced

⅛ teaspoon red pepper flakes

1 can (about 15 ounces) navy beans, rinsed and drained

3 to 4 tablespoons chopped fresh basil

1 tablespoon olive oil

1 tablespoon balsamic vinegar

¾ teaspoon salt

½ teaspoon liquid smoke (optional)

1. Heat oil in Dutch oven over medium-high heat. Add bell pepper; cook and stir 4 minutes or until edges are browned. Add garlic; cook and stir 15 seconds. Add water, tomatoes, zucchini and pepper flakes. Bring to a boil over high heat. Reduce heat; cover and simmer 20 minutes.

2. Add beans, basil, oil, vinegar, salt and liquid smoke, if desired. Remove from heat. Let stand, covered, 10 minutes before serving.

Makes 5 servings

Vegetable Minestrone Soup

2 tablespoons olive or vegetable oil

2 medium zucchini, cut in half lengthwise and thickly sliced (about 3 cups)

2 cloves garlic, minced

½ teaspoon dried rosemary leaves, crushed

4 cups SWANSON® Vegetable Broth (Regular *or* Certified Organic)

1 can (about 14½ ounces) diced tomatoes, drained

1 can (about 19 ounces) white kidney beans (cannellini), rinsed and drained

½ cup uncooked corkscrew-shaped pasta (rotini)

¼ cup grated Parmesan cheese (optional)

1. Heat the oil in a 6-quart saucepot. Add the zucchini, garlic and rosemary and cook until the zucchini is tender-crisp.

2. Stir the broth and tomatoes into the saucepot and heat to a boil. Reduce the heat to low. Cover and cook for 10 minutes.

3. Increase the heat to medium. Stir in the beans and pasta. Cook for 10 minutes or until the pasta is tender. Serve with the cheese, if desired.

Makes 8 servings

Prep Time: 10 minutes
Cook Time: 30 minutes

Tomato-Herb Soup

1 can (about 14 ounces) diced tomatoes
1 can (about 14 ounces) reduced-sodium chicken or vegetable broth
½ cup water
1 bag (8 ounces) frozen bell pepper stir-fry mixture
1 cup frozen green beans
1 tablespoon ketchup
1 to 2 teaspoons dried oregano
1 teaspoon dried basil
⅛ teaspoon red pepper flakes (optional)
1 tablespoon olive oil
½ teaspoon salt

1. Combine tomatoes, broth, water, bell peppers, green beans, ketchup, oregano, basil and pepper flakes, if desired, in large saucepan. Bring to a boil over high heat. Reduce heat; cover and simmer 20 minutes or until beans are tender and mixture has thickened slightly.

2. Remove from heat. Stir in oil and salt. Let stand 5 minutes before serving.

Makes 4 servings

Variation: Substitute chopped fresh bell peppers for the frozen stir-fry mix.

 Tip

When herbs are dried, their oils become more pungent. Before adding dried herbs to a mixture, intensify their flavor by crushing them between your fingers or with the back of a spoon to release their oils.

Twice-Baked Potato Soup

6 large baking potatoes, scrubbed and pricked with a fork
2 tablespoons butter
1 small sweet onion, finely chopped (about ½ cup)
5 cups SWANSON® Chicken Broth (Regular, Natural Goodness™
    or Certified Organic)
¼ cup light cream
1 tablespoon chopped fresh chives
    Potato Toppers

1. Heat the oven to 425°F. Arrange the potatoes on a rack and bake for 30 minutes or until tender. Place the potatoes in a bowl with a lid and let steam. Remove the skin and mash the pulp.

2. Heat the butter in a 3-quart saucepan. Add the onion and cook until tender. Add the broth and **5 cups** of the potato pulp.

3. Place ⅓ of the broth mixture into an electric blender or food processor container. Cover and blend until smooth. Place in a medium bowl. Repeat the blending process with the remaining broth mixture. Return all of the puréed mixture into the saucepan. Stir in the cream and chives and cook for 5 minutes more. Season to taste.

4. Place ¼ **cup** of the remaining pulp mixture in each of 8 serving bowls. Divide the broth mixture among the bowls. Serve with one or more Potato Toppers.   *Makes 8 servings*

Potato Toppers: Cooked crumbled bacon, shredded Cheddar cheese **and/or** sour cream.

Time-Saving Tip: Microwave the potatoes on HIGH for 10 to 12 minutes or until fork-tender.

Prep Time: 10 minutes
Cook Time: 45 minutes

Twice-Baked Potato Soup

Split Pea Soup

1 package (16 ounces) dried green or yellow split peas

1 pound smoked pork hocks *or* 4 ounces smoked sausage links, sliced
    and quartered *or* 1 meaty ham bone

7 cups water

1 medium onion, chopped

2 medium carrots, chopped

¾ teaspoon salt

½ teaspoon dried basil

¼ teaspoon dried oregano

¼ teaspoon black pepper

1. Rinse and sort peas, discarding any debris or blemished peas.

2. Combine peas, pork, water, onion, carrots, salt, basil, oregano and pepper in Dutch oven. Bring to a boil over high heat. Reduce heat to medium-low; simmer, uncovered, 1 hour 15 minutes or until peas are tender, stirring occasionally. Stir frequently near end of cooking to keep soup from scorching.

3. Remove pork; cool. Cut meat into bite-size pieces.

4. Place 3 cups hot soup in food processor or blender; process until smooth.

5. Return puréed soup and meat to Dutch oven. If soup is too thick, add a little water until desired consistency is reached. Heat through.

Makes 6 servings

Split Pea Soup

Easy Mushroom Soup

1¾ cups SWANSON® Beef Broth (Regular, 50% Less Sodium *or* Certified Organic)

1¾ cups SWANSON® Chicken Broth (Regular, Natural Goodness® *or* Certified Organic)

⅛ teaspoon ground black pepper

⅛ teaspoon dried rosemary leaves, crushed

8 ounces fresh mushrooms, sliced (about 2 cups)

¼ cup thinly sliced carrots

¼ cup finely chopped onion

¼ cup sliced celery

¼ cup fresh or frozen peas

1 tablespoon sliced green onion

1. Heat the broth, black pepper, rosemary, mushrooms, carrots, onion, celery and peas in a 4-quart saucepan over medium heat to a boil. Reduce the heat to low. Cover and cook for 15 minutes.

2. Add the green onion. Cook for 5 minutes more or until the vegetables are tender. *Makes 4 servings*

Prep Time: 15 minutes
Cook Time: 25 minutes

Tip

Wipe mushrooms with a damp paper towel or gently brush with a mushroom brush to remove the dirt. Never soak mushrooms in water because they absorb water and will become mushy. Trim and discard the stem ends before using.

Easy Mushroom Soup

Zucchini Soup with Herbed Cream

½ cup sour cream
4 teaspoons chopped fresh basil leaves
4 teaspoons chopped fresh oregano leaves
2 tablespoons olive oil
1 large onion, finely chopped (about 1 cup)
1 clove garlic, minced
4 medium zucchini, thinly sliced (about 10 cups)
¼ teaspoon ground black pepper
3 cups SWANSON® Vegetable Broth (Regular *or* Certified Organic)

1. Stir the sour cream, **1 teaspoon** of the basil and **1 teaspoon** of the oregano in a small bowl. Cover and refrigerate.

2. Heat the oil in a 4-quart saucepan over medium heat. Add the onion and garlic. Cook until tender. Add the zucchini and black pepper. Cook for about 5 minutes or until tender.

3. Add the broth, remaining basil and oregano. Heat to a boil. Reduce the heat to low. Cover and cook for 15 minutes.

4. Place ⅓ of the zucchini mixture into an electric blender or food processor container. Cover and blend until smooth. Pour the mixture into a large bowl. Repeat the blending process twice more with the remaining zucchini mixture. Return all of the puréed mixture to the saucepan. Cook over medium heat for 5 minutes or until hot.

5. Divide the soup among **6** serving bowls. Add about 1 tablespoon of the sour cream mixture into each, using a spoon to swirl the cream on the soup surface. *Makes 6 servings*

Prep Time: 15 minutes
Cook Time: 30 minutes

Vegetable Barley Soup

1 tablespoon vegetable oil
1 to 1½ pounds beef shank cross-cuts
2 medium onions, divided
6 cups water
2 parsnips, peeled and chopped
4 stalks celery, chopped, divided
6 sprigs fresh parsley
2 teaspoons salt
6 black peppercorns
½ pound fresh green beans, cut into 1-inch pieces
4 medium carrots, cut diagonally into ¼-inch-thick slices
½ cup uncooked quick-cooking barley
¼ teaspoon dried tarragon
¼ teaspoon black pepper
1 bay leaf
½ cup frozen corn
½ cup frozen peas
½ cup chopped fresh parsley

1. Heat oil in Dutch oven over medium-high heat. Add beef; cook and stir until browned. Remove from heat.

2. Trim top and root from 1 onion, leaving most of the dried outer skin intact; cut into wedges.

3. Add water, onion wedges, parsnips, half of celery, parsley sprigs, salt and peppercorns to Dutch oven. Bring to a boil over high heat. Reduce heat to medium-low; simmer, uncovered, 1½ hours or until meat is tender, skimming foam that rises to surface.

4. Remove beef from soup and let cool slightly. Strain soup through large sieve or colander set over large saucepan. Press vegetables lightly with slotted spoon to remove extra liquid; discard vegetables.

5. Let stand 5 minutes to allow fat to rise. Skim off fat and discard.

6. Chop remaining onion. Add chopped onion and remaining celery, green beans, carrots, barley, tarragon, black pepper and bay leaf to soup. Bring to a boil over high heat. Reduce heat to medium-low; simmer, uncovered, 15 minutes or until vegetables and barley are tender.

7. Meanwhile, cut meat from bones; discard bones and gristle. Cut meat into bite-size pieces. Stir meat, corn and peas into soup; bring to a boil. Discard bay leaf. Stir in chopped parsley.   *Makes 6 servings*

Corn & Red Pepper Soup

2 tablespoons butter
2 cups coarsely chopped red bell peppers
1 medium onion, thinly sliced
2 cups reduced-sodium chicken or vegetable broth
1 package (10 ounces) frozen corn
½ teaspoon ground cumin
½ cup sour cream
  Salt and white pepper
  Sunflower kernels (optional)

1. Melt butter in large saucepan over medium heat. Add bell peppers and onion; cook and stir until tender.

2. Add broth, corn and cumin; bring to a boil over high heat. Reduce heat to low; cover and simmer 20 minutes or until corn is tender. Cool slightly.

3. Working in batches, process soup in food processor or blender until smooth. Pour into sieve set over bowl; press mixture with rubber spatula to extract all liquid.* Discard pulp. Return liquid to saucepan; whisk in sour cream until evenly blended. Season with salt and white pepper.

4. Cook over low heat until heated through. *Do not boil.* Garnish with sunflower kernels.   *Makes 4 servings*

Omit straining, if desired. Return puréed soup to pan. Proceed as directed.

Roasted Tomato & Barley Soup

1 can (28 ounces) diced tomatoes, undrained
1 large onion, chopped (about 2 cups)
2 cloves garlic, minced
2 tablespoons olive oil
4 cups SWANSON® Chicken Broth (Regular, Natural Goodness™ *or* Certified Organic)
2 stalks celery, diced (about 1 cup)
½ cup uncooked pearl barley
2 tablespoons chopped fresh parsley

1. Heat the oven to 425°F. Drain the tomatoes, reserving the juice. Put the tomatoes, onion and garlic in a 17×11-inch roasting pan. Pour the oil over the vegetables and toss to coat. Bake for 25 minutes.

2. Put the roasted vegetables in a 3-quart saucepan. Add the reserved tomato juice, broth, celery and barley. Heat to a boil. Reduce the heat to low. Cover and cook for 35 minutes or until the barley is tender. Stir in the parsley.

Makes 8 servings

Wild Rice Soup

½ cup dried lentils
1 package (6 ounces) long grain and wild rice blend
1 can (about 14 ounces) vegetable broth
1 package (10 ounces) frozen mixed vegetables
1 cup milk
2 slices (1 ounce each) American cheese, cut into pieces

1. Rinse and sort lentils, discarding any debris or blemished lentils. Place lentils in small saucepan; cover with about 3 cups water. Bring to a boil. Reduce heat to low; cover and simmer 5 minutes. Let stand, covered, 1 hour. Drain and rinse lentils.

2. Cook rice according to package directions in medium saucepan. Add lentils and remaining ingredients. Bring to a boil. Reduce heat to low; simmer, uncovered, 20 minutes.

Makes 6 servings

Roasted Tomato & Barley Soup

Pumpkin Soup with Crumbled Bacon and Toasted Pumpkin Seeds

2 teaspoons olive oil

½ cup raw pumpkin seeds

1 medium onion, chopped

1 teaspoon kosher salt

½ teaspoon chopped dried chipotle pepper, or more to taste

½ teaspoon black pepper

2 cans (29 ounces each) solid-pack pumpkin

4 cups chicken or vegetable broth

¾ cup apple cider

½ cup whipping cream

Sour cream (optional)

3 slices thick-sliced bacon, crisp-cooked and crumbled

Slow Cooker Directions

1. Heat oil in medium skillet over medium heat. Add pumpkin seeds; cook and stir 1 minute or until seeds begin to pop. Transfer to small bowl; set aside.

2. Add onion to same skillet; cook and stir over medium heat until translucent. Stir in salt, chipotle pepper and black pepper. Transfer to slow cooker. Whisk in pumpkin, broth and apple cider until smooth. Cover; cook on HIGH 4 hours.

3. Turn off slow cooker. Whisk in whipping cream. Season to taste with additional salt and black pepper. Strain and keep warm until ready to serve. Garnish with sour cream, toasted pumpkin seeds and crumbled bacon.

Makes 4 to 6 servings

Tip: Pumpkin seeds (or "pepitas") are a common ingredient in Mexican cooking. They can be purchased raw or roasted and salted; either variety may be found hulled or whole.

Pumpkin Soup with Crumbled Bacon
and Toasted Pumpkin Seeds

Cheesy Spinach Soup

1 tablespoon soft reduced calorie margarine
¼ cup chopped onions
2 cups fat-free milk
½ pound (8 ounces) VELVEETA® Made With 2% Milk Reduced Fat
    Pasteurized Prepared Cheese Product, cut into ½-inch cubes
1 package (10 ounces) frozen chopped spinach, cooked, well drained
⅛ teaspoon ground nutmeg
    Dash pepper

1. Melt margarine in medium saucepan on medium heat. Add onions; cook and stir until tender.

2. Add remaining ingredients; cook on low heat until VELVEETA® is melted and soup is heated through, stirring occasionally.

Makes 4 servings, about 1 cup each

Substitute: Prepare as directed, substituting frozen chopped broccoli for the spinach.

Use Your Microwave: Microwave onions and margarine in medium microwavable bowl on high 30 seconds to 1 minute or until onions are tender. Stir in remaining ingredients. Microwave 6 to 8 minutes or until VELVEETA® is completely melted and soup is heated through, stirring every 3 minutes.

Prep Time: 15 minutes
Total Time: 25 minutes

Sweet Potato & Pecan Soup

2 tablespoons unsalted butter
1 large sweet onion, chopped (about 2 cups)
4 cloves garlic, minced
6 cups SWANSON® Vegetable Broth (Regular *or* Certified Organic)
2 bay leaves
3 large sweet potatoes, peeled and cut into cubes (about 6 cups)
¼ teaspoon ground black pepper
1 cup heavy cream, divided
3 tablespoons thinly sliced fresh chives
1 cup pecans, toasted

1. Heat the butter in a 6-quart saucepot over medium heat. Add the onion and garlic and cook until the onions are tender. Add the broth, bay leaves, potatoes and black pepper. Heat to a boil. Reduce the heat to low. Cover and cook for 20 minutes or until the potatoes are tender. Discard the bay leaves. Add ½ **cup** of the cream and heat through.

2. Place ⅓ of the broth mixture in an electric blender or food processor container. Cover and blend until smooth. Pour the mixture into a large bowl. Repeat the blending process twice more with the remaining broth mixture. Return all of the puréed mixture to the saucepot. Cook over medium heat for 5 minutes or until hot. Season to taste.

3. Prepare the *Chive Chantilly.* Beat the remaining heavy cream in a medium bowl with an electric mixer on high speed until stiff peaks form. Gently stir in chives. Serve with the soup and sprinkle with the pecans.

Makes 8 servings

Kitchen Tip: To toast pecans, spread them in a single layer on a jelly-roll pan. Bake at 300°F. for 15 minutes or until the pecans are toasted. Cool and use as directed above.

Prep Time: 30 minutes
Cook Time: 30 minutes

Oven-Roasted Onion Soup

¼ cup (½ stick) butter
3 large yellow onions, thinly sliced
1 teaspoon salt
½ teaspoon black pepper
6 cups reduced-sodium beef broth
½ cup brewed coffee
¼ cup dry sherry
1 baguette, cut into 12 (½-inch) slices
1 cup (4 ounces) grated Swiss cheese
4 sprigs thyme

1. Preheat oven to 325°F. Melt butter in Dutch oven over medium heat. Add onions, salt and pepper. Cook and stir about 10 minutes or until onions are golden but not browned. Cover and bake 45 minutes, stirring once.

2. Stir in broth; cover and bake 30 minutes. Remove from oven; stir in coffee and sherry. Bring soup to a simmer over medium heat. Remove from heat.

3. Place bread slices on baking sheet. Bake until lightly browned on both sides, turning once.

4. Preheat broiler and ladle soup into 4 ovenproof bowls. Top each serving with 2 to 3 slices of toast and 1 tablespoon Swiss cheese.

5. Place bowls in large baking pan; broil 2 to 3 minutes or until cheese is melted and bubbly. Garnish with thyme. *Makes 4 servings*

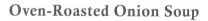

Beans

& Legumes

* * *

Greens, White Bean and Barley Soup

2 tablespoons olive oil
½ pound carrots, diced
1½ cups chopped onions
2 cloves garlic, minced
1½ cups sliced mushrooms
6 cups vegetable broth
2 cups cooked barley
1 can (about 15 ounces) Great Northern beans, rinsed and drained
2 bay leaves
1 teaspoon sugar
1 teaspoon dried thyme
7 cups stemmed chopped collard greens (about 24 ounces)
1 tablespoon white wine vinegar
   Hot pepper sauce
   Red bell pepper strips (optional)

1. Heat oil in Dutch oven over medium heat. Add carrots, onions and garlic; cook and stir 3 minutes. Add mushrooms; cook and stir 5 minutes or until carrots are tender.

2. Add broth, barley, beans, bay leaves, sugar and thyme. Bring to a boil over high heat. Reduce heat; cover and simmer 5 minutes. Add greens; simmer 10 minutes. Remove and discard bay leaves. Stir in vinegar. Season to taste with pepper sauce. Garnish with red bell peppers.   *Makes 8 servings*

Hearty Bean & Barley Soup

   1 tablespoon olive oil
   2 large carrots, chopped (about 1 cup)
   2 stalks celery, sliced (about 1 cup)
   1 medium onion, chopped (about 1 cup)
3½ cups SWANSON® Vegetable Broth (Regular *or* Certified Organic)
   1 can (about 15 ounces) red kidney beans, rinsed and drained
   1 can (14½ ounces) diced tomatoes
   ¼ cup uncooked pearl barley
   2 cups firmly packed chopped fresh spinach leaves
   Ground black pepper

1. Heat the oil in a 4-quart saucepan over medium-high heat. Add the carrots, celery and onion. Cook and stir until vegetables are tender.

2. Stir in the broth, beans, tomatoes and barley. Heat to a boil. Reduce the heat to low. Cover and cook for 30 minutes or until the barley is done.

3. Stir in the spinach and season to taste with black pepper. Cook until the spinach is tender.   *Makes 6 servings*

Barley and Lentil Soup

   8 cups SWANSON® Beef Broth (Regular, Lower Sodium *or* Certified
      Organic)
   2 cloves garlic, minced
   1 teaspoon dried oregano leaves, crushed
   4 large carrots, sliced (about 3 cups)
   1 medium onion, chopped (about 1 cup)
   ½ cup dried lentils
   ½ cup uncooked pearl barley

1. Stir the broth, garlic, oregano, carrots, onion, lentils and barley in a 3½-to 6-quart slow cooker.

2. Cover and cook on LOW for 8 to 9 hours* or until the beans and barley are tender.   *Makes 8 servings*

Or on HIGH for 4 to 5 hours

Hearty Bean & Barley Soup

French Peasant Soup

1 slice bacon, chopped
½ cup diced carrots
½ cup diced celery
¼ cup minced onion
1 clove garlic, minced
2 tablespoons white wine or water
1 can (about 14 ounces) vegetable broth
1 sprig fresh thyme *or* 1 teaspoon dried thyme
1 bay leaf
1 sprig fresh parsley *or* 1 teaspoon dried parsley
½ cup chopped green beans (½-inch pieces)
2 tablespoons uncooked small pasta or elbow macaroni
½ cup canned cannellini beans, rinsed and drained
½ cup diced zucchini
¼ cup chopped leek
2 teaspoons prepared pesto sauce
2 tablespoons grated Parmesan cheese

1. Cook bacon in medium saucepan over medium heat 3 minutes or until partially cooked. Add carrots, celery, onion and garlic; cook 5 minutes or until carrots are crisp-tender. Stir in wine; simmer until most of wine has evaporated. Add broth, thyme, bay leaf and parsley; simmer 10 minutes.

2. Add green beans; simmer 5 minutes. Add pasta; cook 5 to 7 minutes or until almost tender.

3. Add cannellini beans, zucchini and leek; cook 3 to 5 minutes or until vegetables are tender.

4. Remove and discard bay leaf. Ladle soup into 2 bowls. Stir 1 teaspoon pesto into each bowl and sprinkle with cheese. *Makes 2 servings*

Pasta Fagioli

1 jar (1 pound 10 ounces) RAGÚ® Chunky Gardenstyle Pasta Sauce
1 can (19 ounces) white kidney beans, rinsed and drained
1 box (10 ounces) frozen chopped spinach, thawed
8 ounces ditalini pasta, cooked and drained (reserve 2 cups pasta water)

1. In 6-quart saucepot, combine Ragú Pasta Sauce, beans, spinach, pasta and reserved pasta water; heat through.

2. Season, if desired, with salt, ground black pepper and grated Parmesan cheese. *Makes 4 servings*

Prep Time: 20 minutes
Cook Time: 10 minutes

Easy Vegetarian Vegetable Bean Soup

3 cans (about 14 ounces each) vegetable broth
2 cups cubed unpeeled potatoes
2 cups sliced leeks, white part only (about 3 medium)
1 can (about 14 ounces) diced tomatoes
1 medium onion, chopped
1 cup chopped or shredded cabbage
1 cup sliced celery
1 cup sliced carrots
3 cloves garlic, chopped
⅛ teaspoon dried rosemary
1 can (about 15 ounces) white beans, drained
    Salt and black pepper

Slow Cooker Directions
1. Combine broth, potatoes, leeks, tomatoes, onion, cabbage, celery, carrots, garlic and rosemary in slow cooker. Cover; cook on LOW 8 hours.

2. Stir in beans and season with salt and pepper. Cover; cook on LOW about 30 minutes or until beans are heated through. *Makes 10 servings*

Pasta Fagioli

Country Sausage and Bean Soup

2 cans (about 14 ounces each) reduced-sodium chicken broth
1½ cups hot water
1 cup dried black beans, rinsed and sorted
1 cup chopped yellow onion
2 bay leaves
⅛ teaspoon ground red pepper
6 ounces bulk pork sausage
1 cup chopped tomato
1 tablespoon chili powder
1 tablespoon Worcestershire sauce
2 teaspoons olive oil
1½ teaspoons ground cumin
½ teaspoon salt
¼ cup chopped fresh cilantro

Slow Cooker Directions

1. Combine broth, water, beans, onion, bay leaves and red pepper in slow cooker. Cover; cook on LOW 8 hours or on HIGH 4 hours.

2. Brown sausage in large skillet over medium heat, stirring to break up meat. Drain fat.

3. Add sausage, tomato, chili powder, Worcestershire sauce, oil, cumin and salt to slow cooker. Cover; cook on HIGH 15 minutes. Remove and discard bay leaves. Ladle soup into bowls; sprinkle with cilantro.

Makes 8 servings

Lentil and Root Vegetable Stew

    2 cans (about 14 ounces each) chicken broth
1½ cups diced turnip
    1 cup dried red lentils, rinsed and sorted
    1 medium onion, cut into ½-inch wedges
    2 medium carrots, cut into 1-inch pieces
    1 medium red bell pepper, cut into 1-inch pieces
    ½ teaspoon dried oregano
    ⅛ teaspoon red pepper flakes
    1 tablespoon olive oil
    ½ teaspoon salt
    4 slices bacon, crisp-cooked and crumbled
    ½ cup finely chopped green onions

Slow Cooker Directions

1. Combine broth, turnip, lentils, onion, carrots, bell pepper, oregano and pepper flakes in slow cooker. Cover; cook on LOW 6 hours or on HIGH 3 hours or until lentils are tender.

2. Stir in oil and salt. Sprinkle with bacon and green onions.

Makes 8 servings

Veg•All® Black Bean Soup

    1 package (14 ounces) smoked sausage, cut into ½-inch slices
    2 cans (15 ounces each) VEG•ALL® Original Mixed Vegetables
    2 cans (15 ounces each) black beans with spices, drained and rinsed
    2 cans (14½ ounces) chicken broth

In large soup kettle, lightly brown sausage. Add Veg•All, beans and chicken broth; heat until hot. Serve immediately.   *Makes 4 to 6 servings*

Lentil and Root Vegetable Stew

Smoky Navy Bean Soup

2½ tablespoons olive oil, divided
  4 ounces Canadian bacon or ham, diced
  1 cup diced onions
  1 large carrot, thinly sliced
  1 stalk celery, thinly sliced
  3 cups water
  6 ounces red potatoes, diced
  2 bay leaves
¼ teaspoon dried tarragon
  1 can (about 15 ounces) navy beans, rinsed and drained
1½ teaspoons liquid smoke
  ½ teaspoon salt
  ½ teaspoon black pepper

1. Heat 1 tablespoon oil in Dutch oven over medium-high heat. Add bacon; cook 2 minutes or until brown. Remove and set aside.

2. Add onions, carrot and celery to Dutch oven; cook and stir 4 minutes or until onions are translucent. Add water; bring to a boil over high heat. Add potatoes, bay leaves and tarragon; return to a boil. Reduce heat; cover and simmer 20 minutes or until potatoes are tender. Remove from heat.

3. Stir in beans, bacon, remaining 1½ tablespoons oil, liquid smoke, salt and pepper. Remove and discard bay leaves; let stand 10 minutes before serving.

Makes 6 servings

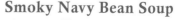

Sausage, Butter Beans and Cabbage Soup

  2 tablespoons butter, divided
  1 large onion, chopped
  12 ounces smoked sausage such as kielbasa or andouille, cut into ½-inch slices
  8 cups chicken broth
  ½ head savoy cabbage, coarsely shredded
  3 tablespoons tomato paste
  1 bay leaf
  4 medium tomatoes, chopped
  2 cans (about 15 ounces each) butter beans, drained
     Salt and black pepper

Slow Cooker Directions

1. Melt 1 tablespoon butter in large skillet over medium heat. Add onion; cook and stir 3 to 4 minutes or until golden. Place in slow cooker.

2. Melt remaining 1 tablespoon butter in same skillet; cook sausage until brown. Add to slow cooker.

3. Place broth, cabbage, tomato paste and bay leaf in slow cooker; stir until well blended. Cover; cook on LOW 4 hours or HIGH 2 hours.

4. Add tomatoes and beans; season with salt and pepper. Cover; cook 1 hour until heated through. Remove and discard bay leaf.   *Makes 6 servings*

Tip: Savoy cabbage is an excellent cooking cabbage with a full head of crinkled leaves varying from dark to pale green. If you can't find savoy cabbage, substitute green cabbage.

Lentil Soup

  2 tablespoons olive oil
  1 medium onion, chopped
  1 medium carrot, chopped
  3 quarts chicken broth
  1 jar (1 pound 10 ounces) RAGÚ® Light Pasta sauce
  1½ cups uncooked lentils, rinsed and drained
  2 cups coarsely shredded fresh spinach or escarole

1. In 6-quart saucepot, heat olive oil over medium-high heat and cook onion and carrot, stirring occasionally, 4 minutes or until vegetables are golden.

2. Stir in broth, Ragú Pasta Sauce and lentils. Bring to a boil over high heat. Reduce heat to low and simmer, stirring occasionally, 30 minutes or until lentils are tender. Stir in spinach and cook an additional 10 minutes or until spinach is tender.

Makes 3½ quarts soup

Prep Time: 15 minutes
Cook Time: 50 minutes

Winter's Best Bean Soup

  6 ounces bacon, diced
10 cups chicken broth
  3 cans (about 15 ounces each) Great Northern beans, drained
  1 can (about 14 ounces) diced tomatoes
  1 large onion, chopped
  1 package (10 ounces) frozen sliced *or* diced carrots
  2 teaspoons minced garlic
  1 fresh rosemary sprig *or* 1 teaspoon dried rosemary
  1 teaspoon black pepper

Slow Cooker Directions
1. Cook bacon in medium skillet over medium-high heat until just cooked; drain and transfer to slow cooker. Add remaining ingredients.

2. Cover; cook on LOW 8 hours. Remove rosemary sprig before serving.

Makes 8 to 10 servings

Serving Suggestion: Place slices of toasted Italian bread in bottom of individual soup bowls. Drizzle with olive oil. Pour soup over bread and serve.

Prep Time: 15 minutes
Cook Time: 8 hours (LOW)

Grandma Ruth's Minestrone

1 pound ground beef
1 can (about 15 ounces) red beans, rinsed and drained
1 package (16 ounces) frozen mixed vegetables
2 cans (8 ounces each) tomato sauce
1 can (about 14 ounces) diced tomatoes
¼ head shredded cabbage (about 2 cups)
1 cup chopped onions
1 cup chopped celery
½ cup chopped fresh parsley
1 tablespoon dried basil
1 tablespoon Italian seasoning
1 teaspoon salt
1 teaspoon black pepper
1 cup cooked macaroni

Slow Cooker Directions

1. Brown beef in large skillet over medium-high heat, stirring to break up meat. Drain fat. Combine beef and beans in slow cooker. Cover; cook on HIGH 2 hours.

2. Stir in remaining ingredients except macaroni. Cover; cook on LOW 6 to 8 hours.

3. Stir in macaroni. Cover; cook on HIGH 30 minutes.   *Makes 4 servings*

Country Bean Soup

1¼ cups dried navy beans or lima beans, rinsed and drained
¼ pound salt pork or fully cooked ham, chopped
¼ cup chopped onion
½ teaspoon dried oregano
¼ teaspoon salt
¼ teaspoon ground ginger
¼ teaspoon dried sage
¼ teaspoon black pepper
2 cups milk
2 tablespoons butter

1. Place navy beans in large saucepan; add enough water to cover beans. Bring to a boil; reduce heat and simmer 2 minutes. Remove from heat; cover and let stand for 1 hour. (Or, cover beans with water and soak overnight.)

2. Drain beans and return to saucepan. Stir in 2½ cups water, salt pork, onion, oregano, salt, ginger, sage and pepper. Bring to a boil. Reduce heat; cover and simmer 2 to 2½ hours or until beans are tender. (If necessary, add more water during cooking.) Stir in milk and butter; cook until mixture is heated through and butter is melted.   *Makes 6 servings*

Lentil Soup with Ham

3½ cups chicken broth
1 pound ham slice or ham steak, trimmed and cut into bite-size pieces
1 cup dried brown lentils, rinsed and drained
1 medium carrot, peeled and diced
½ medium onion, chopped (about ¾ cup)
1 medium jalapeño pepper, seeded and finely chopped
1 teaspoon dried thyme

Combine all ingredients in Dutch oven; bring to boil over high heat. Reduce heat; cover and simmer 30 minutes or until lentils are tender. Let stand, covered, about 15 minutes before serving.   *Makes 4 servings*

Country Bean Soup

Southwestern Chicken & White Bean Soup

1 tablespoon vegetable oil

1 pound skinless boneless chicken breasts, cut into 1-inch pieces

1¾ cups SWANSON® Chicken Broth (Regular, Natural Goodness™
   or Certified Organic)

1 cup PACE® Chunky Salsa

3 cloves garlic, minced

2 teaspoons ground cumin

1 can (about 16 ounces) small white beans, rinsed and drained

1 cup frozen whole kernel corn

1 large onion, chopped (about 1 cup)

1. Heat the oil in a 10-inch skillet over medium-high heat. Add the chicken
and cook until it's well browned on all sides, stirring often.

2. Stir the broth, salsa, garlic, cumin, beans, corn and onion in a 3½-quart
slow cooker. Add the chicken.

3. Cover and cook on LOW for 8 to 10 hours* or until the chicken is cooked
through.   *Makes 6 servings*

Or on HIGH 4 to 5 hours.

Prep Time: 15 minutes
Cook Time: 8 to 10 hours, 5 minutes

Bisques & Chowders

***

Shrimp and Pepper Bisque

1 bag (12 ounces) frozen bell pepper stir-fry mix, thawed

8 ounces frozen cauliflower florets, thawed

2 cups chicken broth

1 stalk celery, sliced

1 tablespoon seafood seasoning

½ teaspoon dried thyme

12 ounces medium raw shrimp, peeled

2 cups half-and-half

2 to 3 green onions, finely chopped

Slow Cooker Directions

1. Combine stir-fry mix, cauliflower, broth, celery, seasoning and thyme in slow cooker. Cover; cook on LOW 8 hours or on HIGH 4 hours.

2. Stir in shrimp. Cover and cook 15 minutes or until shrimp are pink and opaque. Purée soup in batches in blender or food processor. Return to slow cooker. Stir in half-and-half. Ladle into bowls and sprinkle with green onions.
Makes 4 servings

Tip: For a creamier, smoother consistency, strain soup through several layers of damp cheesecloth.

Prep Time: 10 minutes
Cook Time: 8 hours (LOW) or 4 hours (HIGH)

Simply Special Seafood Chowder

1 tablespoon olive or vegetable oil

1 medium bulb fennel, trimmed, cut in half and thinly sliced (about 2 cups)

1 medium onion, chopped (about ½ cup)

1 teaspoon dried thyme leaves, crushed

5 cups water

1¾ cups **SWANSON®** Vegetable Broth (Regular *or* Certified Organic)

1 can (10¾ ounces) **CAMPBELL'S®** Condensed Tomato Soup

1 package (10 ounces) frozen baby whole carrots, thawed (about 1½ cups)

½ **pound fresh *or* thawed frozen firm white fish fillets (cod, haddock *or* halibut), cut into 2-inch pieces**

½ **pound fresh large shrimp, shelled and deveined**

¾ **pound mussels (about 12), well scrubbed**

Freshly ground black pepper

1. Heat the oil in a 4-quart saucepot over medium heat. Add the fennel, onion and thyme and cook until the vegetables are tender. Stir in the water, broth, soup and carrots and heat to a boil.

2. Stir in the fish. Cook for 2 minutes. Stir in the shrimp and mussels. Cover and reduce the heat to low. Cook for 3 minutes or until the fish flakes easily when tested with a fork, the shrimp turn pink and the mussels open. Discard any mussels that do not open.

3. Serve the soup with black pepper. *Makes 6 servings*

Prep Time: 10 minutes
Cook Time: 20 minutes

Broccoli Cream Soup with Green Onions

 1 tablespoon olive oil
 2 cups chopped onions
 1 pound fresh or frozen broccoli florets or spears
 2 cups reduced-sodium chicken or vegetable broth
 6 tablespoons cream cheese
 1 cup milk
 ⅛ teaspoon ground red pepper
 ¾ teaspoon salt
 ⅓ cup finely chopped green onions

1. Heat oil in Dutch oven over medium-high heat. Add onions; cook and stir 4 minutes or until translucent. Add broccoli and broth; bring to a boil over high heat. Reduce heat; cover and simmer 10 minutes or until broccoli is tender.

2. Purée soup in batches in blender or food processor. Return puréed soup to Dutch oven over medium heat. Whisk in cream cheese until melted. Stir in milk, red pepper and salt. Cook 2 minutes or until heated through. Top with green onions.   *Makes 4 servings*

Tip

Once you stir a milk product into a hot soup, heat it gently and only until the mixture is warmed through. Allowing the mixture to boil will cause curdling.

Chicken and Corn Chowder

  1 tablespoon olive oil
  1 pound boneless skinless chicken breasts, cut into ½-inch pieces
  3 cups thawed frozen corn
  ¾ cup coarsely chopped onion (about 1 medium)
  1 to 2 tablespoons water
  1 cup diced carrots
  2 tablespoons finely chopped jalapeño pepper* (optional)
  ½ teaspoon dried oregano
  ¼ teaspoon dried thyme
  3 cups reduced-sodium chicken broth
1½ cups milk
  ½ teaspoon salt

*Jalapeño peppers can sting and irritate the skin, so wear rubber gloves when handling peppers and do not touch your eyes.

1. Heat oil in large nonstick saucepan over medium heat. Add chicken; cook and stir about 10 minutes or until browned and no longer pink in center. Remove chicken.

2. Add corn and onion to saucepan; cook and stir about 5 minutes or until onion is tender. Place 1 cup corn mixture in food processor or blender. Process until finely chopped, adding 1 to 2 tablespoons water to liquify mixture.

3. Add carrots, jalapeño, if desired, oregano and thyme to saucepan; cook and stir about 5 minutes or until corn begins to brown. Return chicken to saucepan. Stir in broth, milk, chopped corn mixture and salt; bring to a boil. Reduce heat to low; cover and simmer 15 to 20 minutes.

Makes 4 servings

Chicken and Corn Chowder

New England Fisherman's Skillet

⅛ teaspoon dried thyme, crushed
½ pound halibut or other firm white fish
2 tablespoons vegetable oil
1 medium onion, chopped
1 clove garlic, crushed
3 tablespoons all-purpose flour
3½ cups reduced-sodium chicken broth
1 can (15¼ ounces) DEL MONTE® Whole Kernel Golden Sweet Corn,
   undrained
1 can (14½ ounces) DEL MONTE® Whole New Potatoes, drained and
   chopped

1. Sprinkle thyme over both sides of fish. In large saucepan, cook fish in
1 tablespoon hot oil over medium-high heat until fish flakes easily when
tested with a fork. Remove fish from saucepan; set aside.

2. Heat remaining 1 tablespoon oil in same saucepan over medium heat. Add
onion and garlic; cook until onion is tender. Stir in flour; cook 1 minute. Stir
in broth; cook until thickened, stirring occasionally. Stir in corn and potatoes.

3. Discard skin and bones from fish; cut fish into bite-sized pieces.

4. Add fish to soup just before serving; heat through. Stir in chopped parsley
or sliced green onions, if desired. *Makes 4 to 6 servings*

Prep Time: 5 minutes
Cook Time: 12 minutes

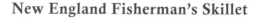

Deep Bayou Chowder

1 tablespoon olive oil
1½ cups chopped onions
1 large green bell pepper, chopped
1 large carrot, chopped
½ pound red potatoes, diced
1 cup frozen corn
1 cup water
½ teaspoon dried thyme
2 cups milk
2 tablespoons chopped parsley
1½ teaspoons seafood seasoning
¾ teaspoon salt

1. Heat oil in Dutch oven over medium-high heat. Add onions, pepper and carrot; cook and stir 4 minutes or until onions are translucent.

2. Add potatoes, corn, water and thyme; bring to a boil over high heat. Reduce heat; cover and simmer 15 minutes or until potatoes are tender. Stir in milk, parsley, seasoning and salt. Cook 5 minutes or until heated through.

Makes 6 servings

Tip

To save an oversalted soup, add a peeled, thinly sliced raw potato and simmer for 10 to 15 minutes. Remove the potato before serving the soup.

Sweet Potato Bisque

1 pound sweet potatoes, peeled and cut into 2-inch chunks
2 teaspoons butter
½ cup finely chopped onion
1 teaspoon curry powder
½ teaspoon ground coriander
¼ teaspoon salt
⅔ cup unsweetened apple juice
1 cup buttermilk
¼ cup water
　　Fresh snipped chives (optional)
　　Plain yogurt (optional)

1. Place potatoes in large saucepan; cover with water. Bring to a boil over high heat. Cook, uncovered, 15 minutes or until potatoes are fork-tender. Drain; cool under cold running water.

2. Meanwhile, melt butter in medium saucepan over medium heat. Add onion; cook and stir 2 minutes. Stir in curry, coriander and salt; cook and stir about 1 minute or until onion is tender. Remove saucepan from heat; stir in apple juice.

3. Combine potatoes, buttermilk and onion mixture in food processor or blender; cover and process until smooth. Pour mixture back into large saucepan; stir in ¼ cup water, if needed, to thin to desired consistency. Cook and stir over medium heat until heated through. *Do not boil.* Garnish with chives and yogurt.　　　　　　　　　　　　*Makes 4 servings*

Cheddared Farmhouse Chowder

1½ cups milk or evaporated milk
1 can (10¾ ounces) condensed cream of mushroom soup, undiluted
1 bag (16 ounces) frozen corn, carrots and broccoli, thawed
2 medium baking potatoes, cut into ½-inch cubes
½ teaspoon dried thyme
¼ teaspoon black pepper
⅛ teaspoon ground red pepper (optional)
½ cup frozen peas, thawed
¼ teaspoon salt
3 ounces sharp Cheddar cheese, shredded or cubed

1. Combine milk and soup in large saucepan; whisk until well blended. Bring to a boil over medium-high heat, stirring frequently.

2. Add mixed vegetables, potatoes, thyme, black pepper and ground red pepper, if desired; return to a boil. Reduce heat; cover and simmer 15 minutes or until carrots are just tender, stirring frequently.

3. Remove from heat; stir in peas and salt. Let stand 5 minutes for flavors to blend. Ladle soup into bowls. Top each serving with cheese.

Makes 5 servings

Tip

Shredded cheese makes a simple and delicious garnish. Or, try dropping small cubes of cheese into the soup. The cubes will melt, adding texture and distinct flavor to the soup.

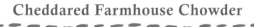

Tomato-Basil Crab Bisque

1 tablespoon butter
½ cup chopped onion
1 can (8 ounces) HUNTS® Tomato Sauce with Roasted Garlic
1 cup half-and-half
1 cup coarsely chopped cooked crab meat
½ cup chicken broth
¼ teaspoon salt
⅛ teaspoon ground black pepper
¼ cup chopped fresh basil leaves

1. Melt butter in a medium saucepan over medium-high heat. Add onion; cook 3 minutes or until tender, stirring frequently.

2. Add tomato sauce, half-and-half, crab, broth, salt and pepper. Bring just to a boil; reduce heat to low. Cover tightly and simmer 5 minutes. Sprinkle with basil before serving. *Makes 4 servings*

Turkey Chowder

2 potatoes, peeled and cubed
1 (10-ounce) package frozen cut green beans
1½ cups water
2 HERB-OX® chicken flavored instant bouillon cubes
½ teaspoon dried basil leaves
½ teaspoon black pepper
1 tablespoon cornstarch
1½ cups milk
2 cups JENNIE-O Turkey Store® Turkey, cooked, cubed

1. In large saucepan over medium-high heat, combine potatoes, beans, water, bouillon, basil and black pepper. Heat to boiling; reduce heat to low. Cover. Simmer 10 minutes or until potatoes are tender, stirring occasionally.

2. Stir together cornstarch and milk. Stir into potato mixture. Cook and stir over medium-high heat 5 minutes or until thickened. Stir in turkey. Cook 2 minutes or until thoroughly heated. *Makes 6 servings*

Tomato-Basil Crab Bisque

Butternut Squash Soup

2 teaspoons olive oil

1 large sweet onion, chopped

1 medium red bell pepper, chopped

2 packages (10 ounces each) frozen puréed butternut squash, thawed

1 can (10¾ ounces) condensed reduced-sodium chicken broth, undiluted

¼ teaspoon ground nutmeg

⅛ teaspoon white pepper

½ cup half-and-half

1. Heat oil in large saucepan over medium-high heat. Add onion and bell pepper; cook 5 minutes, stirring occasionally. Add squash, broth, nutmeg and white pepper. Bring to a boil over high heat. Reduce heat; cover and simmer about 15 minutes or until vegetables are very tender.

2. Purée soup in saucepan with hand-held immersion blender or transfer in batches to food processor or blender. Return soup to saucepan. Stir in half-and-half; heat through. Add additional half-and-half, if necessary, to thin soup to desired consistency.   *Makes 4 servings*

Serving Suggestion: Garnish with a swirl of half-and-half or a sprinkling of fresh parsley.

Chilis & Gumbos

* * *

Country Sausage Chili

2 pounds bulk spicy beef sausage
2 green bell peppers, chopped
2 cups chopped onions
1 tablespoon chopped garlic
2 cans (28 ounces each) crushed tomatoes
2 cans (4 ounces each) diced green chiles, drained
¼ cup chili powder
¼ cup molasses
1 tablespoon brown mustard seeds
2 teaspoons red pepper flakes
1 bay leaf
  Hot pepper sauce

1. Brown sausage in Dutch oven over medium heat, stirring to break up meat. Drain all but 2 tablespoons fat. Stir in bell peppers, onions and garlic; cook and stir about 5 to 8 minutes or until onions are translucent.

2. Add tomatoes, chiles, chili powder, molasses, mustard seeds, pepper flakes, bay leaf and pepper sauce. Simmer about 1 hour or until thickened. Remove and discard bay leaf before serving. *Makes 6 to 8 servings*

Chicken and Sausage Gumbo with Beer

½ cup all-purpose flour
½ cup vegetable oil
4½ cups chicken broth
1 bottle (12 ounces) beer
3 pounds boneless skinless chicken thighs
1½ teaspoons salt, divided
½ teaspoon garlic powder
¾ teaspoon ground red pepper, divided
1 pound fully cooked andouille sausage, cut into ½-inch slices
1 large onion, chopped
½ red bell pepper, chopped
½ green bell pepper, chopped
2 stalks celery, chopped
2 cloves garlic, minced
2 bay leaves
½ teaspoon black pepper
3 cups hot cooked rice
½ cup sliced green onions
1 teaspoon filé powder (optional)

1. Stir together flour and oil in Dutch oven. Cook over medium-low heat, stirring frequently, 20 minutes or until mixture is caramel colored. (Once mixture begins to darken, watch carefully to avoid burning.)

2. Meanwhile, bring broth and beer to a simmer in medium saucepan. Keep warm over low heat. Season chicken with ½ teaspoon salt, garlic powder and ¼ teaspoon ground red pepper.

3. Add chicken, sausage, onion, bell peppers, celery, garlic, bay leaves, black pepper, remaining 1 teaspoon salt and ½ teaspoon ground red pepper to Dutch oven; stir well. Gradually add hot broth mixture, stirring constantly to prevent lumps. Bring to a simmer. Cover and simmer 1 to 2 hours.

4. Remove and discard bay leaves. Place ½ cup rice in each of 6 bowls; top with gumbo. Sprinkle with green onions and filé powder, if desired, before serving. *Makes 6 servings*

Durango Chili

3 tablespoons vegetable oil, divided
1 pound ground beef
1 pound boneless beef top sirloin steak, cut into ½-inch cubes
2 medium onions, chopped
1 green bell pepper, chopped
4 cloves garlic, minced
2 cans (about 14 ounces each) diced tomatoes, undrained
1 can (10¾ ounces) condensed beef broth plus 1 can water
1 bottle (12 ounces) beer
2 cans (4 ounces each) diced green chiles, undrained
¼ cup plus 1 tablespoon chili powder
¼ cup tomato paste
3 to 5 jalapeño peppers,* minced
2 bay leaves
1 teaspoon salt
1 teaspoon ground cumin
½ teaspoon black pepper
2 cans (about 15 ounces each) pinto or kidney beans, rinsed
    and drained
Shredded Cheddar cheese
Sliced green onions

*Jalapeño peppers can sting and irritate the skin, so wear rubber gloves when handling peppers and do not touch your eyes.

1. Heat 1 tablespoon oil in Dutch oven over medium-high heat. Brown ground beef, stirring to break up meat. Add cubed beef; cook, stirring occasionally, until meat is lightly browned. Transfer meat to medium bowl.

2. Heat remaining 2 tablespoons oil in Dutch oven over medium heat. Add onions, bell pepper and garlic; cook until tender. Return meat to Dutch oven. Stir in tomatoes, broth, water, beer, green chiles, chili powder, tomato paste, jalapeños, bay leaves, salt, cumin and black pepper. Bring to a boil. Reduce heat and simmer, partially covered, 2 hours or until meat is very tender. Stir in beans. Simmer, uncovered, until heated through. Remove and discard bay leaves before serving. Top with cheese and green onions.

Makes 6 servings

Durango Chili

Chili Mac in the Slow Cooker

1 pound ground beef or turkey
½ cup chopped onion
1 can (about 14 ounces) diced tomatoes, drained
1 can (8 ounces) tomato sauce
2 tablespoons chili powder
1 teaspoon garlic salt
½ teaspoon ground cumin
¼ teaspoon red pepper flakes
¼ teaspoon black pepper
8 ounces uncooked elbow macaroni
    Shredded Cheddar cheese (optional)

Slow Cooker Directions

1. Brown beef and onion in large skillet over medium heat 6 to 8 minutes, stirring to break up meat. Drain fat.

2. Place beef mixture, tomatoes, tomato sauce, chili powder, garlic salt, cumin, red pepper flakes and black pepper in slow cooker; mix well. Cover; cook on LOW 4 hours.

3. Cook macaroni according to package directions until al dente; drain. Add macaroni to slow cooker; mix well. Cover; cook on LOW 1 hour. Sprinkle with cheese, if desired.   *Makes 4 to 6 servings*

Tip

Chili powder is a spice blend typically made up of ground dried chilies, cloves, coriander, cumin, garlic and oregano.

Chili Mac in the Slow Cooker

Hearty Vegetable Gumbo

1 tablespoon olive oil
½ cup chopped onion
½ cup chopped green bell pepper
¼ cup chopped celery
2 cloves garlic, minced
2 cans (about 14 ounces each) stewed tomatoes
2 cups tomato juice
1 can (about 15 ounces) red beans, rinsed and drained
1 tablespoon chopped fresh parsley
¼ teaspoon dried oregano
¼ teaspoon hot pepper sauce
2 bay leaves
1½ cups uncooked quick-cooking brown rice
1 package (10 ounces) frozen chopped okra, thawed

1. Heat oil in Dutch oven over medium heat. Add onion, bell pepper, celery and garlic; cook and stir 3 minutes or until crisp-tender.

2. Add stewed tomatoes, tomato juice, beans, parsley, oregano, pepper sauce and bay leaves. Bring to a boil over high heat. Stir in rice. Reduce heat to medium-low; cover and simmer 15 minutes or until rice is tender.

3. Add okra; cover and cook 5 minutes or until okra is tender. Remove and discard bay leaves before serving. *Makes 4 servings*

Confetti Chicken Chili

1 pound ground chicken or turkey
1 large onion, chopped
3½ cups reduced-sodium chicken broth
1 can (about 15 ounces) Great Northern beans, rinsed and drained
2 carrots, chopped
1 medium green bell pepper, chopped
2 plum tomatoes, chopped
1 jalapeño pepper, finely chopped (optional)
2 teaspoons chili powder
½ teaspoon ground red pepper

1. Spray large nonstick saucepan with nonstick cooking spray; heat over medium heat. Add chicken and onion; cook and stir 5 minutes or until chicken is browned. Drain fat.

2. Add remaining ingredients to saucepan; bring to a boil. Reduce heat to low; cover and simmer 15 minutes. *Makes 5 servings*

Weeknight Chili

1 pound ground beef or turkey
1 package (1¼ ounces) chili seasoning mix
1 can (about 15 ounces) red kidney beans, rinsed and drained
1 can (about 14 ounces) diced tomatoes with green chiles
1 can (8 ounces) tomato sauce
1 cup (4 ounces) shredded Cheddar cheese
Sliced green onions (optional)

Slow Cooker Directions

1. Brown beef in large skillet over medium-high heat, stirring to break up meat. Drain fat. Stir in seasoning mix.

2. Place beef mixture, beans, tomatoes and tomato sauce in slow cooker. Cover; cook on LOW 4 to 6 hours. Top each serving with cheese and green onions. *Makes 4 servings*

Confetti Chicken Chili

Shrimp and Fish Gumbo

½ pound fresh or thawed frozen orange roughy or other fish fillets

3¾ cups water, divided

  6 ounces medium raw shrimp, peeled and deveined

  1 cup chopped onion

½ cup chopped green bell pepper

  2 cloves garlic, minced

½ teaspoon chicken or fish bouillon granules

  2 cans (about 14 ounces each) stewed tomatoes, drained

1½ cups frozen okra, thawed

  1 teaspoon dried thyme

  1 teaspoon dried savory

¼ teaspoon ground red pepper

⅛ teaspoon black pepper

  2 tablespoons cornstarch

  2 cups hot cooked brown rice

1. Remove and discard skin from fish; cut fish into 1-inch pieces. Bring 3 cups water to a boil in medium saucepan over high heat. Add fish and shrimp; cook 3 to 4 minutes or until fish begins to flake when tested with fork and shrimp are pink and opaque. Drain; set aside.

2. Combine onion, bell pepper, ½ cup water, garlic and bouillon in large saucepan; bring to a boil over medium-high heat. Reduce heat to medium-low; cover and simmer 2 to 3 minutes or until vegetables are crisp-tender.

3. Stir in tomatoes, okra, thyme, savory, red pepper and black pepper; return to a boil. Reduce heat; simmer, uncovered, 3 to 5 minutes or until okra is tender.

4. Combine remaining ¼ cup water and cornstarch in small bowl. Stir into gumbo. Cook and stir over medium heat until mixture boils and thickens. Cook and stir 2 minutes more. Add fish and shrimp; heat through. Serve over rice. *Makes 4 servings*

Simple Turkey Chili

1 pound ground turkey
1 small onion, chopped
1 can (about 28 ounces) diced tomatoes, undrained
1 can (about 15 ounces) black beans, rinsed and drained
1 can (about 15 ounces) chickpeas, rinsed and drained
1 can (about 15 ounces) kidney beans, rinsed and drained
1 can (6 ounces) tomato sauce
1 can (4 ounces) chopped green chiles
1 to 2 tablespoons chili powder

1. Cook turkey and onion in Dutch oven over medium-high heat until turkey is no longer pink, stirring to break up turkey. Drain fat.

2. Stir in remaining ingredients. Bring to a boil. Reduce heat; simmer about 20 minutes, stirring occasionally. *Makes 8 servings*

Chunky Beef Chili

2 tablespoons oil, divided
1½ pounds boneless beef round steak, cut into 1- to 1½-inch pieces
    Salt
1 medium onion, chopped
1 jalapeño pepper,* minced
2 cans (about 14 ounces each) chili-seasoned diced tomatoes

Jalapeño peppers can sting and irritate the skin, so wear rubber gloves when handling peppers and do not touch your eyes.

1. Heat 1 tablespoon oil in large saucepan over medium heat. Brown beef in batches, stirring to break up meat. Remove beef to bowl; season with salt. Drain fat from saucepan.

2. Add remaining 1 tablespoon oil, onion and jalapeño to same saucepan. Cook and stir 5 to 8 minutes or until vegetables are tender. Add beef and any accumulated juices to saucepan. Stir in tomatoes; bring to a boil. Reduce heat; cover and simmer 1¾ to 2¼ hours or until beef is fork-tender.
Makes 4 servings

Simple Turkey Chili

Fresh Tomato Chili

1 tablespoon olive oil

1 small onion, chopped (about 1 cup)

1 clove garlic, minced

1 medium tomato, diced (about 1½ cups)

1 cup frozen corn

1 can (8 ounces) tomato sauce

1 cup canned kidney beans, rinsed and drained

½ to ⅔ cup reduced-sodium chicken or vegetable broth, divided

1 teaspoon chili powder

½ teaspoon ground cumin

¼ teaspoon dried oregano

⅛ teaspoon salt

⅛ teaspoon black pepper

⅛ teaspoon red pepper flakes

1 cup water

1 cup uncooked instant brown rice

1. Heat oil in large nonstick skillet or saucepan over medium-high heat. Add onion and garlic; cook and stir 5 minutes. Add tomato and corn; cook and stir 2 minutes or until tomatoes are pulpy.

2. Add tomato sauce, beans, ½ cup broth, chili powder, cumin, oregano, salt, black pepper and pepper flakes. Simmer 6 to 8 minutes. Add remaining broth if chili is too thick.

3. Meanwhile, bring water to a boil in small saucepan. Add rice. Reduce heat to low; cover and simmer 5 minutes. Remove from heat; let stand 5 minutes. Fluff with fork. Serve chili over rice. *Makes 4 servings*

Chicken Gumbo Ya-Ya

¼ cup all-purpose flour

1 teaspoon dried thyme leaves, crushed

1¾ pounds boneless skinless chicken thighs, cut into 1-inch pieces

2 tablespoons vegetable oil

1 pound smoked sausage, cut into 1-inch pieces

1 can (10¾ ounces) CAMPBELL'S® Condensed Cream of Celery Soup
   (Regular *or* 98% Fat Free)

1 can (10½ ounces) CAMPBELL'S® Condensed Chicken Broth

1 can (about 14½ ounces) diced tomatoes

2 teaspoons hot pepper sauce

1 large onion, chopped (about 1 cup)

1 large green pepper, chopped (about 1 cup)

3 stalks celery, sliced (about 1½ cups)

2 bay leaves

1 package (10 ounces) frozen cut okra, thawed

   Hot cooked rice (optional)

1. Mix the flour and thyme in a gallon-size resealable plastic food storage bag. Add the chicken and shake to coat.

2. Heat the oil in a 12-inch skillet over medium-high heat. Add the chicken and cook until it's well browned, stirring often. Remove the chicken from the skillet. Add the sausage to the skillet and cook until it's well browned, stirring often.

3. Stir the chicken, sausage, soup, broth, tomatoes, hot pepper sauce, onion, green pepper, celery, bay leaves and okra in a 6-quart slow cooker.

4. Cover and cook on LOW for 8 to 9 hours* or until the chicken is cooked through. Remove the bay leaves. Serve with the rice, if desired.

Makes 8 servings

*Or on HIGH for 4 to 5 hours.

Kitchen Tip: You can also stir ½ **pound** of cooked medium shrimp in the cooker during the last 30 minutes of cooking.

Prep Time: 20 minutes
Cook Time: 8 hours

Grilled Steak Chili

¼ cup minced garlic

¼ cup corn oil

3 cups chopped onions

3 cans (about 14 ounces each) Mexican-style diced tomatoes with chiles, undrained

2 cans (about 14 ounces each) crushed tomatoes

2 cups beef broth

¼ cup plus 2 tablespoons chili powder

2 teaspoons ground cumin

2 teaspoons dried oregano

1 teaspoon black pepper

4 pounds beef steak (preferably ribeye)

¼ cup masa harina (corn flour) or yellow cornmeal (optional)

Minced cilantro, sliced green onions and sliced ripe olives (optional)

1. Combine garlic and oil in Dutch oven over low heat; cook 1 minute. Add onion; cook and stir over medium heat 5 minutes. Stir in tomatoes, broth, chili powder, cumin, oregano and pepper. Bring to a boil, stirring occasionally. Reduce heat; cover and simmer 1 to 2 hours or until thick.

2. Preheat grill or broiler. Grill steak about 8 minutes or until just browned on both sides. Let stand 15 minutes. Cut steak into 2½-inch strips on rimmed cutting board. Stir steak and accumulated juices into chili; cook 5 to 10 minutes. For thicker chili, slowly add masa harina; cook and stir 12 to 15 minutes or until thickened. Garnish with cilantro, green onions and olives. *Makes 10 to 12 servings*

Grilled Steak Chili

The publisher would like to thank the companies and organizations listed below for the use of their recipes and photographs in this publication.

Courtesy of The Beef Checkoff

Campbell Soup Company

ConAgra Foods, Inc.

Delmarva Poultry Industry, Inc.

Del Monte Corporation

Dole Food Company, Inc.

Jennie-O Turkey Store, LLC

VELVEETA is a registered trademark of Kraft Foods

Ortega®, A Division of B&G Foods, Inc.

Riviana Foods Inc.

Unilever

Veg•All®

VOLUME MEASUREMENTS (dry)

$1/8$ teaspoon = 0.5 mL
$1/4$ teaspoon = 1 mL
$1/2$ teaspoon = 2 mL
$3/4$ teaspoon = 4 mL
1 teaspoon = 5 mL
1 tablespoon = 15 mL
2 tablespoons = 30 mL
$1/4$ cup = 60 mL
$1/3$ cup = 75 mL
$1/2$ cup = 125 mL
$2/3$ cup = 150 mL
$3/4$ cup = 175 mL
1 cup = 250 mL
2 cups = 1 pint = 500 mL
3 cups = 750 mL
4 cups = 1 quart = 1 L

VOLUME MEASUREMENTS (fluid)

1 fluid ounce (2 tablespoons) = 30 mL
4 fluid ounces ($1/2$ cup) = 125 mL
8 fluid ounces (1 cup) = 250 mL
12 fluid ounces ($1 1/2$ cups) = 375 mL
16 fluid ounces (2 cups) = 500 mL

WEIGHTS (mass)

$1/2$ ounce = 15 g
1 ounce = 30 g
3 ounces = 90 g
4 ounces = 120 g
8 ounces = 225 g
10 ounces = 285 g
12 ounces = 360 g
16 ounces = 1 pound = 450 g

DIMENSIONS

$1/16$ inch = 2 mm
$1/8$ inch = 3 mm
$1/4$ inch = 6 mm
$1/2$ inch = 1.5 cm
$3/4$ inch = 2 cm
1 inch = 2.5 cm

OVEN TEMPERATURES

250°F = 120°C
275°F = 140°C
300°F = 150°C
325°F = 160°C
350°F = 180°C
375°F = 190°C
400°F = 200°C
425°F = 220°C
450°F = 230°C

BAKING PAN SIZES

Utensil	Size in Inches/Quarts	Metric Volume	Size in Centimeters
Baking or Cake Pan (square or rectangular)	8×8×2	2 L	20×20×5
	9×9×2	2.5 L	23×23×5
	12×8×2	3 L	30×20×5
	13×9×2	3.5 L	33×23×5
Loaf Pan	8×4×3	1.5 L	20×10×7
	9×5×3	2 L	23×13×7
Round Layer Cake Pan	8×1½	1.2 L	20×4
	9×1½	1.5 L	23×4
Pie Plate	8×1¼	750 mL	20×3
	9×1¼	1 L	23×3
Baking Dish or Casserole	1 quart	1 L	—
	1½ quart	1.5 L	—
	2 quart	2 L	—